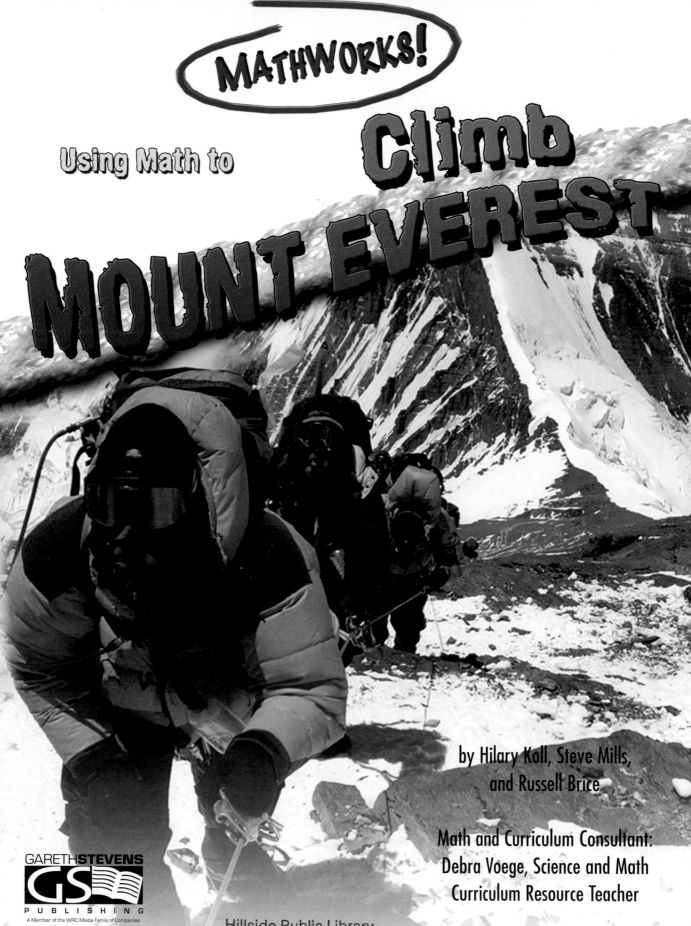

MATHWORKS!

Using Math to

Climb
MOUNT EVEREST

by Hilary Koll, Steve Mills,
and Russell Brice

Math and Curriculum Consultant:
Debra Voege, Science and Math
Curriculum Resource Teacher

GARETH STEVENS
GS
PUBLISHING
A Member of the WRC Media Family of Companies

Please visit our web site at: **www.garethstevens.com**
For a free color catalog describing Gareth Stevens Publishing's
list of high-quality books and multimedia programs, call
1-800-542-2595 (USA) or 1-800-387-3178 (Canada).
Gareth Stevens Publishing's fax: (414) 332-3567.

Library of Congress Cataloging-in-Publication Data

Koll, Hilary.
  Using math to climb Mount Everest / Hilary Koll,
  Steve Mills, and Russell Brice. — North American ed.
     p. cm. — (Mathworks!)
  ISBN-10: 0-8368-6765-3 — ISBN-13: 978-0-8368-6765-7 (lib. bdg.)
  ISBN-10: 0-8368-6772-6 — ISBN-13: 978-0-8368-6772-5 (softcover)
   1. Mathematics—Problems, exercises, etc.—Juvenile literature.
  2. Everest, Mount (China and Nepal)—Problems, exercises, etc.
  I. Mills, Steve, 1955- II. Brice, Russell. III. Title. IV. Series.
  QA139.K65 2007
  510.76—dc22   2006044344

This North American edition first published in 2007 by
Gareth Stevens Publishing
A Member of the WRC Media Family of Companies
330 West Olive Street, Suite 100
Milwaukee, Wisconsin 53212

Technical Consultant: Russell Brice
In 1988. Russell Brice was the first person to cross the
infamous Pinnacle of the northeast ridge of Mount Everest.
With over thirty years experience in mountaineering, he has
climbed Everest fourteen times and reached the summit twice.

Gareth Stevens Editors: Dorothy L. Gibbs and Monica Rausch
Gareth Stevens Art Direction: Tammy West

Photo credits (t=top, b=bottom, c=center, l=left, r=right)
Bill Crouse: 4-5, 6-7, 8-9, 12-13, 14-15, 20-21, 22-23, 24-25,
26-27, 29c. Shutterstock: 10-11 (Wang Sanjun), 16-17 (Jason
Maehl). Russell Brice: 17r; 18-19; 24bl, br; 29 both l, both r; 30.
Robert Bosch: 27r.

Printed in the United States of America

1 2 3 4 5 6 7 8 9 10 09 08 07 06

CONTENTS

HAVE FUN WITH MATH

How to Use This Book

Math is important in the daily lives of people everywhere. We use math when we play games, ride bicycles, or go shopping, and everyone uses math at work. Imagine you are a mountain climber, and you are going to climb Mount Everest, the world's highest mountain. You may not realize it, but mountain climbers would use math to plan their expeditions. In this book, you will be able to try lots of exciting math activities, using real-life data and facts about mountain climbing. If you can work with numbers, measurements, shapes, charts, and diagrams, then you could CLIMB MOUNT EVEREST.

How does it feel to climb a mountain?

Grab your climbing gear and find out what it takes to climb a mountain as high as Mount Everest.

Math Activities

The climber's clipboards have math activities for you to try. Get your pencil, ruler, and notebook (for figuring out problems and listing answers).

CLIMBING TO THE SUMMIT

At Advanced Base Camp, you must watch the weather and pick the right moment to set off for the summit. The direction of the wind is important. Wind direction will determine whether your climb is windy or in the shelter of the surrounding mountains, and any little change in wind direction can make a difference. When you leave ABC, you climb up a short, northeast-facing slope to Camp 1 (C1). From there, you head north until you reach the northeast ridge, at about 27,900 feet. You then use a fixed rope to climb up the rest of the northeast ridge to the summit. Three other camps are between C1 and the summit.

Climber's File

Use the compass pictured below to answer these questions about directions.

These questions will help you practice using a compass.

1) If you are facing north, which direction will you face if you turn
   a) 90° clockwise?
   b) 90° counterclockwise?
   c) 180°?

2) If you are facing west, which direction will you face if you turn
   a) 90° clockwise?
   b) 90° counterclockwise?
   c) 45° clockwise?

3) If you are facing northeast, which direction will face if you turn
   a) 90° clockwise?
   b) 180°?
   c) 45° counterclockwise?

22

4

NEED HELP?

- **If you are not sure how to do some of the math problems, turn to pages 28 and 29, where you will find lots of tips to help get you started.**

- **Turn to pages 30 and 31 to check your answers. (Try all the activities and challenges before you look at the answers.)**

- **Turn to page 32 for definitions of some words and terms used in this book.**

Math Facts and Data

To complete some of the math activities, you will need information from a DATA BOX that looks like this.

Climbers in a group use a fixed rope to keep them from falling or getting lost.

DATA BOX — Length of Journeys

When climbing Mount Everest, the journey is usually thought of in terms of how long it takes rather than how far it is. Near the summit, one-half mile can take 4 to 5 hours to climb, while further down the mountain, you can climb more than one mile in 1 or 2 hours.

This table shows various stages of the journey from Base Camp to the summit and then back to Advanced Base Camp.

Stage of Journey	Starting and Finishing Altitudes	Distance (miles)	Estimated Time
BC to Interim Camp	17,000 – 19,000 feet	6	5 to 6 hours
Interim Camp to ABC	19,000 – 21,000 feet	6	5 to 6 hours
ABC to Camp 1	21,000 – 23,000 feet	1.25	4 to 5 hours
Camp 1 to Camp 2	23,000 – 24,600 feet	.75	5 to 6 hours
Camp 2 to Camp 3	24,600 – 26,000 feet	.25	3 to 4 hours
Camp 3 to Camp 4	26,000 – 27,230 feet	.5	4 to 5 hours
Camp 4 to Summit	27,230 – 29,035 feet	.75	6 to 7 hours
Summit to Camp 4	29,035 – 27,230 feet	.75	2 to 3 hours
Camp 4 to Camp 3	27,230 – 26,000 feet	.5	1 to 2 hours
Camp 3 to Camp 2	26,000 – 24,600 feet	.25	1 to 2 hours
Camp 2 to Camp 1	24,600 – 23,000 feet	.75	2 to 3 hours
Camp 1 to ABC	23,000 – 21,000 feet	1.25	1 to 2 hours

Math Challenge

Green boxes, like this one, have extra math questions to challenge you. Give them a try!

Sunburn Fact

At the top of Mount Everest, the air is much clearer and less polluted than at sea level, so more ultraviolet (UV) light reaches you. UV light also reflects off the snow. Because UV light causes sunburn, you must take care to protect your face, especially around your nose and chin. The rest of your body is covered with protective clothing, so you need sunscreen lotion only on your face and neck.

Math Challenge

The table in the DATA BOX above shows the distances between different camps on the way to Mount Everest's summit and back.

1) What is the distance in kilometers from
   a) BC to Interim Camp?   b) Camp 4 to the summit?

2) Write the descent distances as fractions.

3) Which of the descent distances is written as a mixed number?

You will find lots of amazing details about mountain climbing in FACT boxes that look like this.

23

KNOW THE MOUNTAIN

A group of people from all over the world is on an expedition to try to climb Mount Everest, the highest mountain on Earth. You have a lot of experience climbing high mountains, so you have been invited to join the group. You don't know very much about Mount Everest, so you decide learn more. You must find out how high it is, where it is located, how far it is from where you live, and so on. Each person going on the expedition receives a map showing where Mount Everest is and how far it is from different cities in the world.

Climber's File

In the DATA BOX on page 7, you will see information about some of the highest mountains in the world. Use the information to answer these questions. Give your answers in feet.

1) How high is Mount Everest?

2) Which mountain is the fourth highest mountain in the world?

3) How much higher is Mount Everest than
   a) Kanchenjunga?   e) K2?
   b) Dhaulagiri?   f) Lhotse?
   c) Makalu?   g) Cho Oyu?
   d) Manaslu?

Height Facts

Mount Everest's height was first calculated as 29,002 feet. In 1955, however, scientists used more sophisticated methods of measuring. Mount Everest is now known to be exactly 29,035 feet to the very top rock, with about 11.5 feet of snow on top. Before scientists proved that Mount Everest was the highest mountain in the world, K2 was thought to be the highest.

Name Facts

Did you know Mount Everest has several diferent names?
- The Tibetan name is *Qomolongma* (pronounced Cho-mo-lung-ma). It means "Mother Goddess of the World."
- The Nepalese name is *Sagarmatha* (pronounced Sa-gar-math-a). It means "Forehead of the Ocean" or "Goddess of the Sky."

The World's Highest Mountains

The mountains in this table are the eight highest mountains in the world.
All of these mountains are in the Himalayas, a mountain range in Asia.

Mountain	Other Names	Height (feet)	Height (meters)	Country
Mount Everest	Qomolongma, Sagarmatha	29,035	8,850	Nepal / China (Tibet)
Kanchenjunga		28,169	8,586	Nepal / India (Sikkim)
Dhaulagiri		26,794	8,167	Nepal
Makalu		27,765	8,463	Nepal / China (Tibet)
Manaslu		26,758	8,156	Nepal
K2	Qogir, Godwin Austen	28,250	8,611	Pakistan (Kashmir)
Lhotse		27,940	8,516	Nepal
Cho Oyu		26,906	8,201	Nepal / China (Tibet)

London
4,600 miles

New York
7,600 miles

Tokyo
3,300 miles

Mount Everest

The distances on the map show approximately how far each city is from Mount Everest.

Buenos Aires
10,300 miles

Cape Town
6,200 miles

Sydney
6,100 miles

Climbing Mount Everest is the ultimate goal of many mountain climbers.

Math Challenge

The map above shows the approximate distances, in miles, from Mount Everest to some major cities of the world.

How far is it, in kilometers, from Mount Everest to

1) London?
2) Tokyo?
3) New York?

4) Cape Town?
5) Buenos Aires?
6) Sydney?

KNOW THE MOUNTAIN'S HISTORY

If you are going to climb Mount Everest, you should know its history. Mount Everest has fascinated people for a long time. In the past, people did not want to climb mountains. Some people believed mountains were frightening places where gods and monsters lived. In more recent times, however, people have come to love mountains and enjoy climbing. As the highest mountain in the world, Mount Everest offers a special challenge, and, each year, several thousand climbers, from all over the world, try to reach its summit. Most attempts are made in April or May, when the weather is best for climbing.

Mount Everest

Climber's File

In the DATA BOX on page 9, you will find a time line showing information about the history of Mount Everest. Use the time line to help you answer these questions.

1) In which year was the mountain named Mount Everest?

2) How many years after Mount Everest was named
   a) was the first expedition to the north side?
   b) was the first expedition to the south side?
   c) was the summit first reached?

3) How many years after Edmund Hillary and Tenzing Norgay reached the summit
   a) did the first woman reach the summit?
   b) was the first ascent made without oxygen?
   c) was the first solo ascent made?

History Fact

George Mallory and Sandy Irvine set out for the summit of Mount Everest on June 8, 1924. They wanted to be the first to reach it. They were last seen in the distance by Noel Odell, the expedition leader, but they never returned. Mallory's body was found frozen in the ice more than seventy years later, but no one knows whether he ever reached the summit.

DATA BOX Mount Everest Time Line

George Everest, the British Surveyor General of India in the early 1800s, predicted and measured the heights of mountains in the Himalayas. Mount Everest was named after him in 1865. It was previously known as Peak XV (Peak 15).

Junko Tabei, of Japan, became the first woman to reach Mount Everest's summit on May 16, 1975.

Dr. Edouard Wyss-Dunant led the first expedition to the south side of Mount Everest in 1952.

Reinhold Messner and Peter Habeler made the first ascent of Mount Everest without oxygen on May 8, 1978.

| 1865 | 1921 | 1952 1953 | 1975 | 1978 1980 |

Charles Howard-Bury led the first expedition to the north side of Mount Everest in 1921.

Chris Bonnington led the first ascent of Mount Everest's southwest face on September 24, 1975.

Edmund Hillary and Sherpa leader Tenzing Norgay were the first to reach Mount Everest's summit on May 29, 1953.

Reinhold Messner made the first solo ascent of Mount Everest on August 20, 1980.

Balloon Fact

In October 1991, an expedition of two hot-air balloons sailed over Mount Everest. Both balloons nearly met with disaster. One balloon had problems with its burners, and the other ran out of the gas it needed to slow its descent.

Math Challenge

How many days after May 16, 1975, when Junko Tabei reached Mount Everest's summit, did the team led by Chris Bonnington make the first ascent of Mount Everest's southwest face?

FITNESS PROGRAM

To climb to the summit, or highest point, of Mount Everest, you need to be physically fit. Months in advance, you need to start a training program to improve your cardiovascular fitness. You need to strengthen your heart, so it works more efficiently. Running, bicycling, and swimming are all good for cardiovascular fitness. Lifting weights will improve your upper body strength, which you will need for carrying your heavy backpack and for digging out snow holes. You might want to gain some extra weight, too. Some people who try to climb Mount Everest use up their body's fat reserves and run out of energy.

Climber's File

In the DATA BOX on page 11, you will see a schedule for a training plan.

1) If you follow this plan for the whole month of July,
   a) how many days off will you have?
   b) how many days will you run 8 miles?
   c) how far will you run in total?
2) If it takes you about 7 minutes to run each mile, about how long will it take you to run 8 miles?
3) Look at the dates of the days off in July. Identify the pattern these days make.

Fitness Fact

In general, the more physically fit you are, the more you will enjoy climbing. Just being fit, however, does not mean you will be able to cope with high altitudes. A person who is not used to the reduced amount of oxygen in the air is likely to get altitude sickness. During an expedition, climbers often spend long periods of time resting while they get used to new altitudes. Some people are so frustrated by the need for frequent rests that they leave the expedition without attempting to reach the summit. Climbing at high altitudes is physically challenging. Even very fit people sometimes cannot deal with the discomfort and pain involved, so they never reach the summit. Those who are less fit may succeed through sheer determination. Strong willpower can sometimes be more important than fitness.

DATA BOX Training Plan

You decide to train with a running program for one month, running over hills or on a treadmill, carrying a backpack. The calendar below shows the distances you will run each day.

JULY

Monday	Tuesday	Wednesday	Thursday	Friday	Saturday	Sunday
		1 8 miles	2 8 miles	3 8 miles	4 8 miles	~~5~~ DAY
6 8 miles	7 8 miles	8 8 miles	9 8 miles	~~10~~ DAY	11 8 miles	12 8 miles
13 8 miles	14 8 miles	~~15~~ DAY	16 8 miles	17 8 miles	18 8 miles	19 8 miles
~~20~~ DAY	21 8 miles	22 8 miles	23 8 miles	24 8 miles	~~25~~ DAY	26 8 miles
27 8 miles	28 8 miles	29 8 miles	~~30~~ DAY	31 8 miles		

Math Challenge

Use the DATA BOX above to answer the following questions about your running schedule.

1) If you follow this plan for the whole month of July,
   a) how many times will you run on a Friday?
   b) how many times will you run on a Saturday?
   c) on which day of the week will you not have a day off?

2) How many miles will you run in July if the pattern is
   a) run 8 miles a day for 3 days, followed by 2 days off?
   b) run 8 miles a day for 2 days, followed by 1 day off?
   c) run 8 miles every other day?

You need to start making preparations for your journey and choose which items to take with you. Make sure you take high quality equipment because you must be able to rely on it. How much does all your equipment weigh? Your backpack might not feel very heavy at home, but it will be a different story during your climb! If you have been lifting weights, you will find it easier to carry everything. Your expedition will need sleeping tents, a cook tent, a dining tent, a storage tent, and a toilet tent. Luckily, yaks will carry most of the heavy equipment up the mountain, including the tents.

Climber's File

In the DATA BOX on page 13, you will see the climbing equipment you will need to take with you.

How heavy, in total, are
1) the four carabiners?
2) the two tape slings?
3) the sunglasses and the goggles?
4) the ascender and the descender?
5) the large pack and the day pack?

Math Challenge

Use the DATA BOX on page 13 to help you answer this question.

What is the total weight of all the items on the list
1) in ounces?
2) in pounds?

Equipment Facts

- Carabiners are metal clips used to connect pieces of climbing equipment to the safety harness tied around the climber. A carabiner also can be clipped around the safety rope to stop a climber from falling.
- A descender is normally shaped like the number eight. It creates friction on a rope by making it difficult for the rope to pass through freely. The friction helps slow the rope so a climber can control his or her speed when sliding down the rope.

- An ascender is able to slide up a rope, but then it clips in place so it cannot slide back down. Climbers can use ascenders to help them climb up ropes.
- Tape slings are loops of tape about 20 inches long. They are used to connect the various pieces of equipment (ascenders, carabiners, etc.) to a harness.
- Prussic loops are similar to tape slings, but they are made of rope. A climber can use these loops to make an ascender if he or she breaks or loses a metal ascender.

DATA BOX

Equipment List

Climbing Equipment		Weight
Harness	1	14.5 ounces
Carabiners	4	3 ounces each
Descender	1	10 ounces
Ascender	1	10 ounces
Tape Slings	2	0.5 ounce each
Prussic Loop	1	0.5 ounce
Ice Ax	1	18 ounces
Crampons	2	15 ounces each
Head Lamp and Bulbs	1	6 ounces
Pocket Knife	1	4 ounces
Sunglasses	1	2 ounces
Goggles	1	2 ounces
Large Pack	1	30 ounces
Day Pack	1	20 ounces

Equipment Facts

Group Equipment
Cooking stoves, cooking tables, eating tables and chairs, cooking equipment, eating utensils, first aid equipment, radios, a satellite phone, a computer, solar panels, oxygen masks, and oxygen cylinders, or tanks.

Personal Equipment
Camera or camcorder with film and spare batteries, a repair kit, reading materials, a personal first aid kit, a diary and writing materials, sunscreen, lip balm, two water bottles, personal toilet equipment, four headlamp batteries, two sleeping bags, and a foam mat.

Clothing
Five shirts, three jackets, five pairs of pants, two pairs of long underwear, one pair of shorts, five pairs of gloves, a sun hat, a warm hat, ten pairs of socks, plastic climbing boots, hiking boots, and gaiters.

THE JOURNEY TO BASE CAMP

You are now prepared to start your expedition! Everyone in your group flies to Kathmandu, the capital of Nepal. Kathmandu is still far from where you will start climbing Mount Everest. After several days, your group flies to a town called Lhasa before driving on to Base Camp (BC). BC is the first camp on Mount Everest and the place from where you will start the main part of your climb. You will need to stay at Base Camp for one week while you organize your equipment and acclimatize, or get used to the high altitude. At all points on your journey, from Kathmandu to Mount Everest, you must be very careful. The higher in altitude you travel, the more likely you are to feel the effects of altitude sickness.

Climber's File

In the DATA BOX on page 15, you will see a graph showing the percentage of oxygen available at different altitudes. Use the information on the graph to help you answer these questions.

1) At approximately what altitude is the percentage of oxygen
   a) 50%? c) 75%? e) 35%?
   b) 40%? d) 100%?

2) Estimate the percentage of oxygen at
   a) 12,000 feet.   d) 21,000 feet.
   b) 8,000 feet.   e) 22,500 feet.
   c) 25,000 feet.

At Mount Everest's Base Camp, Sherpas level the ground before they pitch the tents.

Altitude Sickness Facts

• If you climb to high altitudes too quickly, you may get acute mountain sickness (AMS). Symptoms of AMS include some or all of the following: headache, tiredness, feeling sick, vomiting, loss of appetite, dizziness, and disturbed sleep. People react to changes in altitude differently, but most people will start feeling mild symptoms of AMS in Lhasa, at 12,000 feet.
• To try to prevent AMS, climbers increase their altitude slowly. Increasing altitude slowly allows the body to acclimatize, or get used to less oxygen being available at higher altitudes. Acclimatization is a slow process that usually takes several days.

DATA BOX | High Altitude

Altitude is the measurement of height above sea level. As you climb, you reach higher altitudes. The higher the altitude, the more likely you are to feel ill or to get acute mountain sickness (AMS). You feel sick because there is less oxygen in each breath you take as you climb higher and higher above sea level.

This graph shows the percentage of oxygen available to breathe at different altitudes.

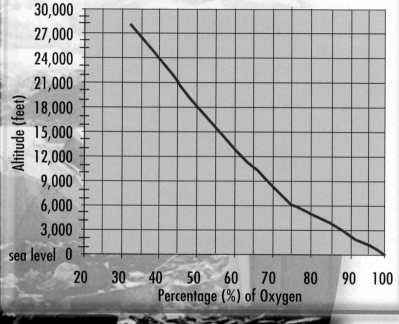

Math Challenge

Use the information in the DATA BOX above to help you answer these questions.

1) Approximately what percentage of oxygen is gained when descending from 18,000 feet to 6,000 feet?

2) Approximately what percentage of oxygen is lost when ascending from 21,000 feet to 24,000 feet?

3) Approximately how many feet have you climbed if the percentage of oxygen drops from 70 percent to 50 percent?

While you are staying at Base Camp for a week, acclimatizing to the high altitude, you prepare for the climb to a point known as Advanced Base Camp (ABC). It is an 11-mile trip to ABC, and you will travel from 17,000 feet to 21,000 feet above sea level. It will take you two days to reach ABC, so you will need to set up another camp halfway to ABC. At Base Camp, you hire yaks to carry all the equipment you need for the rest of the climb. You must make sure you have enough yaks to carry everything. You will also hire experienced yak handlers to take care of the animals.

Climber's File

In the DATA BOX on page 17, you will see information about the yaks you need to carry your equipment to ABC. Use the information to help you answer these questions.

1) How many yak handlers will you need to take care of
   a) 15 yaks?
   b) 24 yaks?
   c) 27 yaks?
   d) 33 yaks?

2) How many yaks will you need to carry
   a) 180 pounds?
   b) 900 pounds?
   c) 4,500 pounds?
   d) 27,000 pounds?

3) How much does it cost to hire three yaks and one yak handler for seven days?

A yak's long hair keeps it warm at high altitudes.

Yak Facts

Yaks have poor vision, so they tend to smell their way along a trail. Because they put their back hooves in the exact same places on the path as their front hooves, they are very sure-footed on difficult ground.

Climbers load yaks with equipment at Base Camp.

DATA BOX ## Know Your Yaks

Yaks carry the heavy equipment climbers need up Mount Everest to make the traveling easier for climbers.

- A yak can carry only 45 pounds on each side of its back, so each yak carries a total of 90 pounds per trip.
- Each yak handler can care for three yaks.
- The cost per day to hire each yak is $11.
- The cost per day to hire each yak handler is $15.

Sherpa Facts

- For each person climbing in an expedition, there is normally a local Sherpa to help. The Sherpas are an ethnic group, living in the high mountain villages of Nepal.
- Since Sherpas live at high altitudes (10,000 to 13,000 feet) from birth, they are naturally acclimatized to those altitudes. Only a small percentage of Sherpas, however, excel at acclimatizing to even higher altitudes, and many Sherpas become just as sick as other people do at higher altitudes.
- Sherpas normally have the day of the week on which they were born as a first name and "Sherpa" as a last name. Since many names are the same, Sherpas are usually called by their name and then by the name of the village from which they come. For example, a Sherpa may be called Nima Sherpa from Thangboche. (*Nima* means "Sunday.")

Math Challenge

Your group's equipment weighs a total of 27,000 pounds.

Use the information in the DATA BOX above to help you find
1) the number of yaks your group needs.
2) the number of yak handlers needed.
3) the cost to hire that number of yaks and yak handlers for one day.
4) the cost to hire that number of yaks and yak handlers for seven days.

KEEPING A JOURNAL

Your group arrives at Advanced Base Camp (ABC), and you set up your tents. The weather is not good. It is very windy, and snow is falling. You will need to stay at ABC until weather conditions improve. Luckily, you brought a journal with you, and, to pass the time, you write notes about what you have been doing each day. You also look through some weather reports you brought about weather conditions on Mount Everest at different times of the year. Now that you are getting ready to make the last big push for the summit, you are starting to feel a little frightened, particularly because it is so cold.

Climber's File

The DATA BOX on page 19 contains a graph of temperatures for different places on your journey. The temperatures are recorded in degrees Celsius (°C). Use the graph to answer these questions.

1) At Base Camp, a temperature of 8 °C fell by 10 °C. What is the new temperature?
2) At the summit, a temperature of −12 °C fell by 5 °C. What is the new temperature?
3) In Lhasa, a temperature of −3 °C rose by 7 °C. What is the new temperature?

Math Challenge

Use the graph in the DATA BOX on page 19 to help you answer these questions.

1) The range is the difference between the minimum and maximum temperatures. What is the approximate range for
   a) Kathmandu in summer? b) Lhasa in winter? c) Base Camp on Mount Everest in winter?
2) What is the difference between the lowest winter temperature in Kathmandu and the lowest winter temperature at Mount Everest's summit?
3) Which location has the greatest range between its winter low and its summer high?

Summer and Winter Temperatures

This graph shows minimum and maximum temperatures in summer and in winter for four locations near and on Mount Everest.

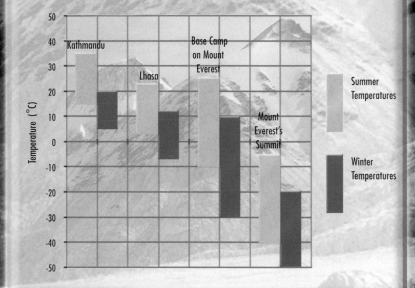

Temperature (°C)

Kathmandu

Lhasa

Base Camp on Mount Everest

Mount Everest's Summit

Summer Temperatures

Winter Temperatures

Wind Fact

The speed of the wind affects the temperature close to your body because wind can blow away the warmer air around you. The effect of wind speed on temperature is called "wind chill."

Altitude Facts

- Kathmandu is 4,500 feet above sea level.
- Lhasa is 12,000 feet above sea level.
- Mount Everest's Base Camp is 17,000 feet above sea level, and its summit is 29,035 feet above sea level.

FOOD AND DRINK

On your last push to the summit, the food you take must be as light as possible, but it also must provide you with lots of energy. You will bring cookies and chocolate and boil-in-the-bag meals. Your body will use 7,000 to 8,000 calories a day on the mountain, so you need to eat as much as you can. Unfortunately, one effect of altitude is that the higher you climb, the less you feel like eating. You also need to make sure you drink enough water so you do not dehydrate. Drinking enough can be a problem. You have to melt ice or snow on a stove before you can have something to drink.

Climber's File

1) The group on your 65-day expedition has 130 people. If each person eats one egg per day, how many eggs does your group need?

2) If about one of every one hundred eggs usually breaks during the journey, how many eggs are likely to break?

3) About how many eggs should you take to make sure you do not run out?

Food Fact

It is much easier to eat and drink at Advanced Base Camp (ABC) than it is in camps higher up on Mount Everest, so it is important to eat well at ABC. At the higher camps, you will eat boil-in-the-bag meals or food that has been precooked at ABC and carried up to the higher camps. Taking precooked meals means you only have to heat up your food rather than cook it completely.

At Advanced Base Camp, all of the water needed for cooking, drinking, washing, and cleaning comes from melted ice.

Toilet Paper Facts

On an expedition to Mount Everest, your group will need lots of toilet paper.

• A person's nose runs more often when climbing to high altitudes, and many climbers use toilet paper as handkerchieves.

• In the high camps, which are camps above Advanced Base Camp, toilet paper is used to clean plates and cups, to mop up spills, and to clean out climbers' oxygen masks when they get clogged.

• Toilet paper is useful in first aid kits, too. It can be used for cleaning wounds and for many other purposes.

• Because toilet paper has so many uses, each person needs about 1½ rolls every day during the climb.

Cooking Facts

• Propane gas is a type of fuel used to cook or heat up food and to melt snow or ice into water for drinking or cleaning. Propane is also used to heat dining tents at Base Camp and Advanced Base Camp. You will need a large supply of propane for an entire expedition.

• To avoid getting carbon monoxide poisoning, do not breathe in fumes or smoke from the stoves when cooking.

Math Challenge

Use the toilet paper facts above to answer this question.

How many rolls of toilet paper will your group of 130 people need on its 65-day expedition?

CLIMBING TO THE SUMMIT

At Advanced Base Camp, you must watch the weather and pick the right moment to set off for the summit. The direction of the wind is important. Wind direction will determine whether your climb is windy or in the shelter of the surrounding mountains, and any little change in wind direction can make a difference. When you leave ABC, you climb up a short, northeast-facing slope to Camp 1 (C1). From there, you head north until you reach the northeast ridge, at about 27,900 feet. You then use a fixed rope to climb up the rest of the northeast ridge to the summit. Three other camps are between C1 and the summit.

Climber's File

Use the compass pictured below to answer these questions about directions.

These questions will help you practice using a compass.

1) If you are facing north, which direction will you face if you turn
   a) 90° clockwise?
   b) 90° counterclockwise?
   c) 180°?

2) If you are facing west, which direction will you face if you turn
   a) 90° clockwise?
   b) 90° counterclockwise?
   c) 45° clockwise?

3) If you are facing northeast, which direction will face if you turn
   a) 90° clockwise?
   b) 180°?
   c) 45° counterclockwise?

DATA BOX Length of Journeys

When climbing Mount Everest, the journey is usually thought of in terms of how long it takes rather than how far it is. Near the summit, one-half mile can take 4 to 5 hours to climb, while further down the mountain, you can climb more than one mile in 1 or 2 hours.

This table shows various stages of the journey from Base Camp to the summit and then back to Advanced Base Camp.

Stage of Journey	Starting and Finishing Altitudes	Distance (miles)	Estimated Time
BC to Interim Camp	17,000 – 19,000 feet	6	5 to 6 hours
Interim Camp to ABC	19,000 – 21,000 feet	6	5 to 6 hours
ABC to Camp 1	21,000 – 23,000 feet	1.25	4 to 5 hours
Camp 1 to Camp 2	23,000 – 24,600 feet	.75	5 to 6 hours
Camp 2 to Camp 3	24,600 – 26,000 feet	.25	3 to 4 hours
Camp 3 to Camp 4	26,000 – 27,230 feet	.5	4 to 5 hours
Camp 4 to Summit	27,230 – 29,035 feet	.75	6 to 7 hours
Summit to Camp 4	29,035 – 27,230 feet	.75	2 to 3 hours
Camp 4 to Camp 3	27,230 – 26,000 feet	.5	1 to 2 hours
Camp 3 to Camp 2	26,000 – 24,600 feet	.25	1 to 2 hours
Camp 2 to Camp 1	24,600 – 23,000 feet	.75	2 to 3 hours
Camp 1 to ABC	23,000 – 21,000 feet	1.25	1 to 2 hours

Sunburn Fact

At the top of Mount Everest, the air is much clearer and less polluted than at sea level, so more ultraviolet (UV) light reaches you. UV light also reflects off the snow. Because UV light causes sunburn, you must take care to protect your face, especially around your nose and chin. The rest of your body is covered with protective clothing, so you need sunscreen lotion only on your face and neck.

Math Challenge

The table in the DATA BOX above shows the distances, in miles, between the different camps on the way to Mount Everest's summit and back.

1) What is the distance in kilometers from
   a) BC to Interim Camp?   b) Camp 4 to the summit?

2) Write the descent distances as fractions.

3) Which of the descent distances is written as a mixed number?

HEART RATE AND BREATHING

The climb to the summit is difficult. Your heart pumps very fast. The air at this altitude has less oxygen, and your body is struggling to get enough. As your heart pumps faster, you may feel sick. A lack of oxygen can also play tricks with people's minds, and they imagine they see things that are not really there. Your breathing is heavy, and you are not sure you are going to be able to make it to the summit. At Camp 3, which is at about 26,000 feet, you start to breathe oxygen from a cylinder, or tank. The oxygen will help you sleep before the final stages of the climb.

Climber's File

In the DATA BOX on page 25, you will see information about how much oxygen a climber uses each hour. Use the information to answer these questions.

1) When sleeping, how many liters of oxygen are used in
   a) 1 minute?　　d) 1 hour?　　　　g) 15 seconds?
   b) 10 minutes?　e) 8 hours?
   c) half an hour?　f) 30 seconds?

2) When climbing, how many liters of oxygen are used in
   a) 1 minute?　　d) 1 hour?　　　　g) 15 seconds?
   b) 10 minutes?　e) 8 hours?
   c) half an hour?　f) 30 seconds?

As climbers reach high altitudes, they must be aware of the possible effects these altitudes can have on themselves or others in the expedition.

Heart Rate and Breathing Facts

- "Resting heart rate" is measured when a person is not doing any exercise and is not at a high altitude. When exercising, a person's muscles need more oxygen so the heart starts pumping more quickly and the heart rate increases. The breathing rate also quickens. At a high altitude, less oxygen is available from the air so both the heart rate and breathing rate need to increase even more to get enough.
- If a climber's oxygen tank runs out of oxygen, his or her body will immediately get much colder, increasing the risk of frostbite. The climber will also move more slowly and might not make it to the next camp. He or she might have to spend a night out in the open, and the added exposure to cold temperatures could result in hypothermia or even death.

Most climbers use oxygen tanks once they reach Camp 3.

DATA BOX Oxygen Tanks

Because oxygen is very expensive — about $400 per cylinder —
it must be used carefully. Oxygen cylinders can be adjusted to
allow the oxygen to flow out at different rates.

When a person is sleeping, the oxygen tank is set at a flow rate of 1 liter per minute. When a person is climbing, the flow rate is set at 2 liters per minute. One cylinder lasts approximately 8 hours at a flow rate of 2 liters per minute. The diagram below shows that each person will use about 5 oxygen cylinders on the journey from Camp 3 to the summit and back.

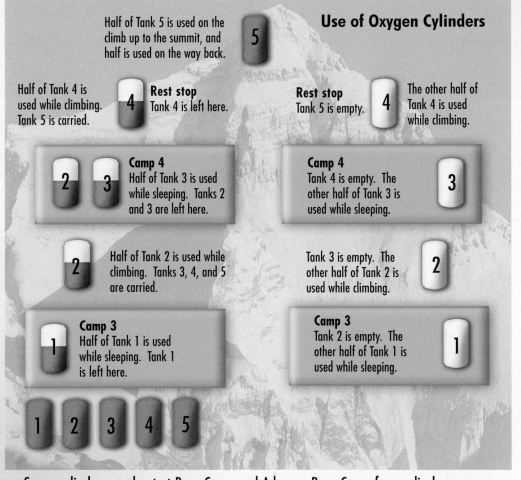

Use of Oxygen Cylinders

Half of Tank 5 is used on the climb up to the summit, and half is used on the way back.

Half of Tank 4 is used while climbing. Tank 5 is carried.

Rest stop
Tank 4 is left here.

Rest stop
Tank 5 is empty.

The other half of Tank 4 is used while climbing.

Camp 4
Half of Tank 3 is used while sleeping. Tanks 2 and 3 are left here.

Camp 4
Tank 4 is empty. The other half of Tank 3 is used while sleeping.

Half of Tank 2 is used while climbing. Tanks 3, 4, and 5 are carried.

Tank 3 is empty. The other half of Tank 2 is used while climbing.

Camp 3
Half of Tank 1 is used while sleeping. Tank 1 is left here.

Camp 3
Tank 2 is empty. The other half of Tank 1 is used while sleeping.

Spare cylinders are kept at Base Camp and Advance Base Camp for medical purposes.

Math Challenge

An oxygen tank was used at the rate of 4 liters per minute for 1 hour, 2 liters per minute for 2 hours, and 1 liter per minute for 8 hours, until it was empty. If the same oxygen tank was used at a rate of 2 liters per minute, how many hours of oxygen would it give?

REACHING THE SUMMIT

Congratulations! You finally made it! You managed to reach the summit of Mount Everest – the highest point on Earth. As you look around, you think of all the other men and women who achieved this goal. You remember Edmund Hillary and Tenzing Norgay who first reached this point at 11:30 a.m. on May 29, 1953. They placed three flags on the summit of Mount Everest: the flags of Great Britain, Nepal, and the United Nations. In early expeditions, most teams going to the summit were representing their countries and were very proud to plant their nations' flags on the summit.

Climber's File

The DATA BOX to the right displays the flags of different countries around the world.

Answer these questions about the flags.

1) What fraction of the area of
   a) the flag of Belgium is black?
   b) the flag of Argentina is blue?
   c) the flag of Libya is green?
   d) the flag of the United States has stripes?

2) Which two flags have about the same proportion of red?

3) What is the name of the shape of Nepal's flag?

A British climber plants his nation's flag on Mount Everest's summit.

DATA BOX

Your Expedition's Flags

Argentina   Belgium   Nepal   Czech Republic

China   Greece   Libya   Austria

U.S.A.   Sudan   Peru   South Africa

The Climbing Experience

"Climbing Mount Everest is very claustrophobic. You wear a lot of clothing, including big boots, big gloves, an oxygen mask, and goggles. The goggles make it hard to see because they fog up each time you breathe. You also wear a headlamp because you often are climbing in the dark. The final part of the climb is very frustrating. You know you are fit and strong, but because of the effects of high altitude, you can take only a few steps at a time. Reaching the summit is really a relief because the climbing is over, and you can turn around and go home. Of course, you have a moment of excitement, but only upon your return to Advanced Base Camp can you relax a little and fully understand and enjoy having reached the summit. One thing is for sure, those who have been to the top of the world have an inner confidence that will last them for the rest of their lives."

— Russell Brice

Math Challenge

Use the DATA BOX on page 26 to help you find approximately what fraction of the area of
1) the flag of the Czech Republic is blue.
2) the flag of Greece is blue.
3) the flag of Sudan is green.
4) the flag of South Africa is red.

MATH TIPS

PAGES 6-7

Climber's File

When subtracting numbers with many digits, make sure you line up all the digits by unit — the tens with the tens, the hundreds with the hundreds, and so on.

Math Challenge

When dividing a number by 5, you can divide it by 10, then double your answer. When multiplying a number by 8, you can double the number, then double your answer, and then double the answer again.

Example: 125 x 8 =
125 doubled = 250   500 doubled = 1000
250 doubled = 500   so 125 x 8 = 1000

Another way of converting miles to kilometers is to multiply the number of miles by 1.6.

PAGES 8-9

Climber's File

TOP TIP: To find the number of years between two dates, subtract the older date from the newer date.

Example: 1936
        − 1865
           71   1936 is 71 years after 1865.

Math Challenge

First, find how many days May 31 falls after May 16. Add to your answer the number of days in June, July, and August. Finally, add to that answer the number of days in September up to the September 24.

PAGES 10-11

TOP TIP: When reading a calendar, look at the column headings to see the days of the week. All of the dates in one column will fall on the week day shown in that column's heading.

PAGES 12-13

Math Challenge

TOP TIP: Remember that 1 pound is equal to 16 ounces. To change ounces to pounds, divide the number of ounces by 16.

PAGES 14-15

Climber's File

To find the altitude for a given oxygen percentage, move straight up from the percentage until you reach the red line, then move across to find the altitude.

To find the oxygen percentage for a given altitude, move across from the altitude until you reach the red line, then move down to find the oxygen percentage.

PAGES 16-17

TOP TIP: To divide a number by 90, first divide the number by 10, then divide your answer by 9.

PAGES 18-19

Climber's File

To find the new temperature when a temperature rises, find the old temperature on the number line (*below*), then move to the right the number of degrees the temperature has risen. To find the new temperature when a temperature falls, move to the left of the old temperature on the number line.

-10 -9 -8 -7 -6 -5 -4 -3 -2 -1 0 1 2 3 4 5 6 7 8 9 10

Math Challenge

To find a minimum temperature, read across from the bottom of a bar. To find a maximum temperature on the graph on page 19, read across from the top of a bar. To find the range, subtract the minimum temperature from the maximum temperature.

PAGES 20–21

Climber's File

You can multiply 130 by 65 in several steps. First, multiply 100 by 65. Then multiply 30 by 65 and add the two answers together.

To multiply a number by 100, move the number's digits two places to the left, and use zeros to fill the empty columns.

Example: $65 \times 100 = 6,500$

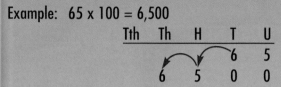

To multiply a number by 30, first multiply the number by 3, then multiply the answer by 10.

To multiply a number by 10, move the number's digits one place to the left, and use a zero to fill the empty column.

Example: $65 \times 10 = 650$

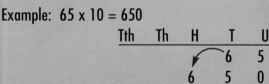

To divide a number by 100, move each of the number's digits two places to the right.

Example: $7,340 \div 100 = 73.4$

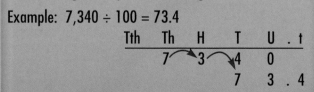

Math Challenge

Multiply 130 by 65. Divide the answer in half. Add the half to the first amount to find your final answer.

PAGES 22–23

Climber's File

An angle is a measure of turn. Angles are measured in degrees. The symbol for degrees is °. One whole turn is 360°. One-fourth of a whole turn is 90°. One half of a 90° turn is 45°.

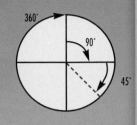

Math Challenge

TOP TIP: A mixed number is a whole number and a fraction.

PAGES 24–25

Math Challenge

First, find how many hours the tank would last if it was used at 1 liter per minute.

4×1 hour $+ 2 \times 2$ hours $+ 1 \times 8$ hours

Divide your answer by 2 to find out how many hours the tank would last if it was used at 2 liters per minute.

PAGES 26–27

1 part of this shape is blue, out of 5 equal parts altogether.
The fraction 1/5 (one fifth) tells you what part of this whole shape is blue.

TOP TIP: To find what fraction of a shape is shaded, find how many equal parts there are altogether (the bottom number of the fraction). Then find how many parts are shaded (the top number of the fraction).

Math Challenge

These flags are split into equal parts to help you.

ANSWERS

PAGES 6–7

Climber's File

1) 29,035 feet   2) Lhotse

3) a) 866 feet   e) 785 feet
   b) 2,241 feet   f) 1,095 feet
   c) 1,270 feet   g) 2,129 feet
   d) 2,277 feet

Math Challenge

1) 7,360 km   4) 9,920 km
2) 5,280 km   5) 16,480 km
3) 12,160 km   6) 9,760 km

PAGES 8–9

Climber's File

1) 1865
2) a) 56 years
   b) 87 years
   c) 88 years
3) a) 22 years
   b) 25 years
   c) 27 years

Math Challenge

131 days

PAGES 10–11

Climber's File

1) a) 6 days   b) 25 days   c) 200 miles
2) 56 minutes off
3) The days off fall on every fifth day.

Math Challenge

1) a) 4 times   b) 3 times   c) Tuesday
2) a) 152 miles   b) 168 miles   c) 128 miles

PAGES 12–13

Climber's File

1) 12 ounces
2) 1 ounce
3) 4 ounces
4) 20 ounces
5) 50 ounces

Math Challenge

1) 160 ounces   2) 10 pounds

PAGES 14–15

Climber's File

1) a) 18,000 feet   d) 0 feet
   b) 24,000 feet   e) 26,000 feet
   c) 6,000 feet

2) a) about 63 percent
   b) about 70 percent
   c) about 38 percent
   d) about 45 percent
   e) about 43 percent

Math Challenge

1) 25 percent
2) 5 percent
3) about 9,500 feet

PAGES 16–17

Climber's File

1) a) 5 handlers   2) a) 2 yaks
   b) 8 handlers   b) 10 yaks
   c) 9 handlers   c) 50 yaks
   d) 11 handlers   d) 300 yaks

3) $336

Math Challenge

1) 300 yaks   3) $4,800
2) 100 handlers   4) $33,600

PAGES 18–19

Climber's File

1) −2 °C   3) 4 °C
2) −17 °C

Math Challenge

1) a) 20 °C   c) 40 °C
   b) 19 °C

2) 55 °C

3) Base Camp

PAGES 20–21

Climber's File

1) 8,450 eggs
2) about 84 or 85 eggs
3) more than 8,534, possibly as many as 9,000 eggs

Math Challenge

12,675 rolls of toilet paper

PAGES 22–23

Climber's File

1) a) east   2) a) north   3) a) southeast
   b) west   b) south   b) southwest
   c) south   c) northwest c) north

Math Challenge

1) a) 9.6 km
   b) 1.2 km
2) $\frac{3}{4}$, $\frac{1}{2}$, $\frac{1}{4}$, $\frac{3}{4}$, and $1\frac{1}{4}$
3) $1\frac{1}{4}$ (the distance from Camp 1 to ABC)

PAGES 24–25

Climber's File

1) a) 1 liter   2) a) 2 liters
   b) 10 liters   b) 20 liters
   c) 30 liters   c) 60 liters
   d) 60 liters   d) 120 liters
   e) 480 liters   e) 960 liters
   f) $\frac{1}{2}$ liter   f) 1 liter
   g) $\frac{1}{4}$ liter   g) $\frac{1}{2}$ liter

Math Challenge

8 hours

PAGES 26–27

Climber's File

1) a) $\frac{1}{3}$ c) $\frac{1}{1}$ or 1
   b) $\frac{2}{3}$ d) $\frac{3}{4}$

2) Austria and Peru

3) pentagon

Math Challenge

1) $\frac{2}{8}$ or $\frac{1}{4}$ 3) $\frac{2}{12}$ or $\frac{1}{6}$
2) just over $\frac{5}{9}$ 4) $\frac{5}{24}$

GLOSSARY

ACCLIMATIZE physically adjust to or get used to a new altitude

ACUTE MOUNTAIN SICKNESS (AMS) an illness people may experience when they reach high altitudes

ADVANCED BASE CAMP (ABC) a rest camp on Mount Everest at 21,000 feet above sea level

ALTITUDE height above sea level

ASCENDER a metal clip that climbers can slide up a rope and then lock into place. Climbers use ascenders to help them climb up ropes.

BASE CAMP (BC) a rest camp on Mount Everest at 17,000 feet above sea level

CARABINERS metal clips used to connect pieces of climbing equipment

CARDIOVASCULAR relating to the heart and to the system that moves blood through the body

COMPASS a tool with a magnetic pointer that always points north

COUNTERCLOCKWISE in the opposite direction from the way a clock's hands turn

CRAMPONS metal frames with spikes on the bottoms. Each frame fits onto the bottom of a hiking boot to provide a better grip on icy ground.

DEHYDRATE to lose water from the body in amounts that endanger health

DESCENDER a metal tool that creates friction on a rope passing through it. A descender helps control the speed at which a climber slides down a rope.

EXPEDITION an organized journey taken by a group of people for a particular purpose

FIXED ROPE a rope that a climbing group's leader attaches to a mountain and leaves in place so other group members can use it to climb up the mountain

FRACTIONS numbers that represent parts of whole numbers or parts of groups

FRICTION a rubbing force that slows down a moving object

FROSTBITE freezing of the skin or other body tissues. Frostbite can cause permanent damage if the skin or tissues are frozen for too long.

GAITERS waterproof coverings that fit over the lower legs and the feet

HYPOTHERMIA a life-threatening condition in which a person's body temperature drops far below normal

INTERIM CAMP a rest camp on Mount Everest, between Base Camp and Advanced Base Camp, at about 19,000 feet above sea level

PROPANE a gas used in camping equipment for heating or cooking

SHERPA a member of an ethnic group living in the Himalaya Mountains in Nepal. Sherpas often serve as expert guides on mountaineering expeditions in the Himalayas.

SUMMIT the highest point

TREADMILL an exercise machine with a moving belt that people run on

YAKS long-haired oxen

Measurement Conversions

1 inch = 2.54 centimeters (cm)
1 foot = 0.3048 meter (m)
1 mile = 1.609 kilometers (km)

1 ounce = 28.33 grams (g)
1 pound = 0.4536 kilogram (kg)
$°F = (°C \times 1.8) + 32°$ $°C = (°F - 32) \div 1.8$